The Favor I Owe the World

By
Patricia A. Fisher

Published by
ITSMEEE™ Industries
Aurora, CO
USA

Patricia A. Fisher

The Favor I Owe the World

Published by ITSMEEE™ Industries

All interior art by Patricia A. Fisher
Book layout and design by Patricia A. Fisher
Book production and technical advice by D. H. Fisher
Editing by D. H. Fisher
Photography by D. H. Fisher
Cover production and design by
NZ Graphics, Lakewood, CO
Letter from Char used by permission
Printed in the United States of America

First Edition

Library of Congress Control Number: 2005900848
Old ISBN: 0-9677231-6-7
New ISBN: 978-0-9677231-6-7

ROSES ARE RED

VIOLETS ARE BLUE

I HAVE A FAVOR

THAT I OWE YOU

Other Titles by
Patricia A. Fisher

With Love ITSMEEE™
Copyright © 1997 by Patricia A. Fisher

With Love ITSMEEE™ II
Copyright © 1998 by Patricia A. Fisher

Introducing Number III, ITSMEEE™
Copyright © 1999 by Patricia A. Fisher

ITSMEEE™ On My Journey Home
Copyright © 1999 by Patricia A. Fisher
ITSMEEE™ Industries

Hello, ITSMEEE™ Again
Copyright © 2002 by Patricia A. Fisher
ITSMEEE™ Industries

ITSMEEE™ Beneath the Grey
An Autobiography
Copyright © 2003 by Patricia A. Fisher
ITSMEEE™ Industries

Other Titles (Continued)
By Patricia A. Fisher

From This Day Forward
Copyright © 2003 by Patricia A. Fisher
ITSMEEE™ Industries

I Want to LIVE!
Copyright © 2004 by Patricia A. Fisher
ITSMEEE™ Industries

Walk a Mile in Our Shoes
Copyright © 2005 by Patricia A. Fisher
ITSMEEE™ Industries

The Favor I Owe the World
Copyright © 2005 by Patricia A. Fisher
ITSMEEE™ Industries

Home Is Where We Park It!
Copyright © 2008 by Pat Fisher
Funhous Publishing

The Absence of Awful
Copyright © 2012 by Patricia A. Fisher
ITSMEEE™ Industries

Table of Contents:

Table of Contents: (continued)

Table of Contents:
(continued)

ROSES ARE RED.

VIOLETS ARE BLUE.

WE HAVE WHAT IT TAKES,

TO SEE US THROUGH.

The day after Family Night I was approached by one of my clients. She stated that she had received a book last night. She went on to state that she had begun to read it.

I was surprised by this information, because this client does not read!

She told me that Pat Fisher had written the book, and she had another 8 books or so that she wanted to collect and read.

I could not believe these words were coming from this client! I encouraged her to get the books and read them.

We checked our meager library, and found 2 more books by Pat Fisher. She quickly checked the books out and left the building smiling, stating that she was going to read them all.

When asked what she liked about the books, she replied, "They are readable. They express feelings that I have never had words for. She knows what it (mental illness) is like, and she writes about it (mental illness) in a way that everyone can understand.

I gotta get her books, and read them all. Can you help me?"

-Karen Terry, MSW, Therapist

Thank you
for letting me
be a part of
your journey.

Patricia A.
Fisher

Whatever It Takes

Most people go on with their lives doing whatever it takes.
This can be anything, from skiing with prostheses, doing artificial insemination, or living a full life with blindness.

Whatever we have to deal with, it appears that we would rather have our own difficulties than someone else's.

I would rather have a mental illness than have my husband's allergies. I would be very scared, if I developed difficulty breathing, or if I started getting his awful headaches.

I go through awful experiences with my mental illness, but I am more familiar with mental illness than I would be with someone else's illness. I hope I can remember this, when I'm in the middle of freaking out.

My mental illness sometimes makes me want to die, but my 'Dennis' told me that his allergies sometimes make him feel the same way.

I would be willing to bet that we all have had a time, when we thought dying might be easier than some awful thing we may be experiencing.

Have you, or someone you knew, ever commented, "I have the flu so bad I either want to get better or die!"

We may wish to die, when someone we love passes away, when our business goes belly up, when we become depressed, or maybe, when we develop a guilty conscience about something we've done.

People I've known along the way are colossal people! They definitely do whatever it takes, as they are living good lives with some very worrisome problems... This list is long. Yet, these people not only manage, but learn to thrive.

We learn to go around or through these possible road blocks. The more I write about our world, the more warriors and survivors I become aware of.

I'm appreciating reality more and more, because of how people create new ways of living with their terrible challenges.

Something else amazes me. When something horrendous happens to one of us, a lot of times, there are good people ready to come to our aid.

Life becomes a case of, "How can this person be helped? How can we make them feel good about themselves again? How can we get them able to contribute to their world?"

I guess we are all in the same boat, or on the same planet... What affects one of us, affects all of us.

In my mind and heart, I can see more and more people who choose to live a life of service. They choose to do this, because they believe in a person having the best life possible. I believe they do whatever it takes, because they not only celebrate life, they honor it.

I have interviewed one such person in the next few pages.

Mr. Wes House, and his beloved wife, Marsha, own and operate the 160 acre, Winding River Resort with the help of their wonderful family and employees.

An Interview with Wes

(1.) What kind of work do you do?

I've a variety of work. As far as a job description, I work with the public, number one, the facilities, the horses and other livestock we have. Yet, in sum total, it's ownership of a resort that caters to people who come for camping, or lodging, and are looking for an outdoor, vacation experience. That may be horseback riding, fishing, hiking and so forth...

(2.) What is your greatest challenge at work?

He chuckles. There's coordination of everything to make harmony. As far as our guests and employees it is the timing of events, and people being punctual around their work duties. I would say that's one of the biggest challenges – to make everything blend. **Does that have a title?** Frustration... **He chuckles again.** No, no title.

(3.) What helps you get up in the morning?

Oh! I love what I do! I have no trouble getting up to face the day, because I enjoy working with the public.

I love the livestock. We have some wonderful employees! So, I just have a love of the work. It's harder to stop than it is to start. **That's fabulous! Not everyone gets that.** No, I'm very blessed! **I think people around here care about you, too. It shows... This place has harmony also. I think...**

(4.) How do you handle anger?

I would not have anger as much as disappointment. After so many years in the business, you see things that may look different than what the situation is...

You may see things on a camp site that may be going on, but when you talk to people, there may be a better reason than you think. **For example?** One of the biggest challenges is extra people coming in, and our watching for those who actually do not belong here. Our facilities are geared toward the number of camp sites and lodging. I guess I should say our water, sewer, and electric, and all those things.

When we do have people come in here and utilize a shower, and sneak out without paying, or double up on a camp sight, those are taking away from those who pay to stay here.

So, that's one thing that can cause anger, but things aren't always as they seem.

You might see people doubling up on a sight, where actually they have rented another sight, but because they had friends, they wanted to be closer, and so they may be two units occupying one sight.

I've always had concern for the people who belong here – for the people who have paid to be here, and who have set aside that one or two weeks as their vacation to have a good quality time.

It does disappoint or anger me, when people come in and take away from that. **They don't have that love of it that you do.**

(5.) What is your definition of love?

Well, you have a lot of different types of love. You have the love of God, the love of family, and my wife. I mean, they all fall into different categories. I assume you are talking about the love of the business.

As far as the business and the property are concerned, there's the enjoyment, comfort, and feeling the confidence about what we're doing.

I believe that I'm meant to be here, in terms of what I'm doing, because of my personality, my background, and my education. All of that has lead up to this point, and I feel like it fits. It's a good fit!

(6.) Do you consider yourself a happy person?

Oh! Yah!

(7.) What percent of the time do you feel good?

A very high percent of the time, I don't know a number to put to that.

(8.) How would you rate your life? Tell me a number between 1 and 10, (10 being best).

Well it's probably an 8 or 9. I don't think anyone has a perfect life. We all look back on some things we'd like to change, but I rate it very high. **I think that's a good rating, because I also don't think we on earth can get a 100% of what we might want.**

(9.) Tell me about your family life.

Well, I have a wonderful wife. She is very supportive and very active in the business. She's a great helpmate!

We share a number of common interests in terms of the live stock, people, sports and so forth.

We have 5 children and 12 grand children. I feel very blessed that we all live in close proximity.

One of the nicest things about our operation here – it lends itself to the young people. As soon as they're 8 or 9 years old, they're out here doing something. Not that they're never here before that, but as far as their work – they're helping with dinners, and setting tables. They're working out on the animal farm. When they get in their teens, they're working in the store, along with supervision.

Quite a few family members work here at Winding River Resort, including a niece from Ohio. **I get such a good feeling when I listen to you talk about your family.** Well, we're just so fortunate to give them this experience. They love the horseback riding. (That's one of the biggest draws). Then, they're learning to be around people just by working in a store... **It's great! It's great! You sort of have a college here for them! We Laugh!**

(10.) If your higher power was right in front of you, what would you say?

Thanks...

(11.) How are you unique? How are you similar to others?

That's an interesting question. Well, I think all of us are unique. I'm not sure I know how to answer that. I might go back to what I said before. I think what I am doing is a good fit for who I am, in terms of my temperament, for my personality, my background or my knowledge. I'm very fortunate to be afforded this opportunity, and in this position, and be able to utilize that. **From what I see, you are unique.**

I'm surrounded with people who have common goals, and similar likes and dislikes.

We have similar beliefs. Maybe, we all surround ourselves with people who fit in with our definition.

(12.) What would be your greatest dream?

I guess my greatest dream, is to see my kids grow up as happy in what they're doing, as I have been able to be...

Winding River

Winding River Resort
Grand Lake, Colorado 80447

This wondrous place
Is a fantasy land
Beyond
My own belief!

There isn't
Any place like it!
I really
Don't want to leave!

A herd of horses
Are brought about
For anyone
To ride.

They stand there
At the stable –
Their beauty
Not denied.

Then, at night,
They're herded back
To where they all
Belong.

Here is where
They eat and sleep.
'Bout them
I write this song.

A little pen
Containing goats
And chickens,
Ducks and pigs.

Right there
On that good land,
Where people
Park there rigs.

A little child,
With smiles galore,
Rides by
Upon a horse.

This is a memory
He will have.
He will come back,
Of course!

Larger groups
Of equestrians
Mount up
To take a ride.

Off they go,
All at once,
Throughout
The countryside.

Lovely cabins
That people rent
Are here and there
Around.

Elk and other
Animals
Are free
To roam the ground.

A great big man –
His name is Wes.
He owns a lot
Or part,

Of this
Magnificent area,
That's so close
To our heart.

I do not know him
Personally,
But when he entered
The place,

I saw a man
Of power,
With goodness
On his face.

It takes this kind
Of person
To work and run
This land.

Where people
Can pitch a tent,
Or camp
In rigs more grand.

I believe
There is a ranch
Not too
Far away.

It's also
"Winding River"
I saw it
Yesterday.

This whole place
Is beautiful!
It's shared
With open hand.

So that
Everybody
May know
And understand,

That there's
No other place like this –
So beautiful
And unique!

I hope that all
The rest of you
Will come
And take a peek.

In a tree,
Where we are parked,
A woodpecker
Made its home.

It pecked a hole
Into a tree,
Where baby birds
Have grown.

Ice cream socials
During the week –
Just adding
To the fun,

So we can
Get together
Where one
Meets everyone!

Chuck wagon breakfasts
Or dinners,
Or, maybe,
A hayride,

Will keep you
Happily busy,
And feeling good
Inside!

I guess I've told you
Most of it –
Of how
I love this place.

Dear God,
Keep it going.
It brings smiles
To our face...

Wes' Challenge and Ours

I asked Wes if he thought his trees would get re-infested with beetles. He said that there is a 50% chance of this happening.

I asked if I could help by writing about it, and informing the public. Maybe a lot of people would donate their time or money for such a cause.

I asked Wes if he was scared. I told him I would be if I had no power over this challenge (like writing to let people know). **Maybe we can save a few trees. (My husband just smiled and called me a tree hugger)... There are worse things I could do.**

I asked Wes if he had any power over a possible re-infestation.

He said that spraying can help you save what you have, but it is 9 or 10 dollars per tree. So, if you look around here, it becomes a point that cannot be pursued because of numbers. People on a small home sight, who have maybe 100 trees, could pursue this.

He said that a lot of people up here go into the spraying business just to get a handle on the problem. Another way is to remove the trees that are dead, to alleviate some of the fuel left on the ground (fire hazard).

This spring he chose this route, and removed 700 visibly affected trees. Not one healthy tree was removed. He has done absolutely no spraying...

Winding River Resort is surrounded almost completely by government ground.

First of all, the property to the South, has done what they can do in terms of removing trees. Rocky Mountain National Park and Arapahoe National Forest border Winding River also.

On federal land, the government lets nature take its course. As a result, more beetles could come flying in, and infect more trees.

Wes doesn't see Winding River as ever being barren. The beetles do not attack the smaller trees. They attack the big mature ones. So, you'll see the smaller ones, and that is good. The smaller trees replace the older ones.

Wes does not have a specific plan, other than what he has already done. He hopes he won't have to bring in that equipment, and take out more trees...

There is a Spruce Beetle problem in the Steamboat Springs area, and in 2 years, it may reach Winding River. Wes will probably spray for that, because he doesn't have that many Spruce Trees (smaller expense).

I thanked Wes, for meeting with me, in the shade of one of those beautiful, old pines.

I would like to let people know what a unique place Winding River Resort is. You might think of it as a ritzy place, when you see the word resort, but it is more than that.

Come experience it for yourself. 'My' Dennis and I have been camping here since it opened in 1972. It just never lost its' charm...

One of my favorite parts of W.R.R. is still the trees and the sound of the wind blowing through them.

Only God Can Make A Tree
(Winding River Continued)

My tears begin to fall, as I look over this magical place. They fall again and again...

I imagine all the beautiful spirits, whose honor it has been to even glance at such pristine beauty.

Millions of tall, friendly pines, grace us with their presence, as they silently reach for clear blue skies.

Yonder mountains, laden with glaciers of snow, reach up through fluffy, white clouds.

Grasses sway among wild flowers and Dandelions, and are anchored to the ground with rich mountain soil.

Breezes play with my hair, and I hear sounds of nature's inhabitants. This orchestra is complete, and each living thing has a part to play.

As my heart tries to capture all of this, my thoughts turn to sadness. For this incredible beauty has been threatened by beetles. These beetles kill Lodgepole Pine Trees at altitudes less than 9300 feet, and the Lodgepole Pines are the predominant trees in much of Colorado's Rocky Mountains...

The last two years have had warmer winters. So, it was not cold enough to kill these beetles as usual. Four or five years ago a draught weakened the trees, which only made the situation worse.

There are more beetles, still destroying the trees, not too far from here. If they are not weeded out, the disease will again spread back to this place.
More trees will have to be sacrificed...

Please, people, there must be a way of saving the remaining trees! Please keep Winding River as unique and magical as it is now!

Please keep its' orchestra playing and pine trees alive.

It takes lifetimes to make a tree, and only God can make one...

My tears have stopped, because I feel there is hope.

I look toward you who love this earth and these mountains. I look toward myself. This way we can stop the tears and prevent new ones. Only then can we save Winding River. Only then can we save a world of hurt... For all of our Rocky Mountain trees may be at risk!

My Dear Readers, please remember, "Only God can make a tree". Yet, you and I might be able to save one...

With Love, Truth, and Respect,

Patricia A. Fisher (Pat)

We want this!

Not this!

I WAS GOING
THE SPEED LIMIT,
AND TOLD
'MY' DENNIS,
"AT LEAST WE WON"T
GET A TICKET."

HE SAID,
"YES, YOU WILL
GET A TICKET!
THEY CAN'T CATCH THE
OTHER GUYS!"

YOU KNOW

YOU ARE GETTING

OLD,

WHEN ALL MEN WANT

FROM YOU,

IS A PLATE OF YOUR

HOMEMADE
NOODLES...

Transformed

Forgive me. For I go along and
live my life loving and being
loved.

My life has not always been an
easy one, as there has been
much discomfort and despair.

I guess you could say I have paid
the piper. I have been deeply
depressed and so full of rage I
could hardly stand it.

I have been very lost, for long
periods of time, and at times, I
have almost taken my own life.

Anger use to live in my heart, and resentment once colored all of my senses. My spent energy went unnoticed, because I saw life through a sort of veil.

Reality, for me, was something to fear, and, for many years, I tried to hide from it.

Equality was always 'not quite there', though I spoke of it often to others.

Being among people made me feel huge discomfort, and I tried to avoid it whenever I could. I thought I was just shy...

My husband's side of the family was always "his", not "mine". In my heart, I felt they were only glad to see him.

I felt invisible for a long, long time. Then I started writing...

As words fell onto the pages, I began to know myself. My secrets were set free, and so was I.

I feel that God speaks to me by way of my writing, and this freedom reminds me of that bible verse, "The truth shall set you free."

As written in my books, my truth let me forgive myself and all others. At the same time, I realized how much the world needs love.

This was when I got even closer to God.

Hence, the old saying,
"God is love", came true for me.

It is a beautiful feeling, to sit among people I previously feared, and have that fear replaced by love.

At these times, there is a bit of levity and a peaceful knowingness. Good feelings spread to everyone in the room, and the ride home is full of satisfying memories.

Equality is found in that space full of love, and every person is important.

Miracles are absolutely everywhere, and I find that loving people takes less energy than being mad at them.

Resentment is replaced by wishes to share. It becomes easy to be in the moment, since fear is less of a problem.

Forgive me. I am no longer the person you use to know. I have been transformed, and am no longer invisible. I walk shoulder to shoulder with my fellow human beings...

Forgive me as I go along and live my life, loving and being loved...

Unconditional Love
What is it?

Is it when people relate to you with love, even when you are at your worst?

Is it when they see only the part of you that is good?

Do they look past your frailties to that which is more pure in you?

Or, do they see it all and love you anyway?

Unconditional love means "no strings attached."

It means you will be loved 'through it all' for as long as you live...

A bible verse speaks of forgiving seventy times seven. This helps me when I am forgiving someone over and over again.

It appears to me, the harder it is to forgive, the more necessary the forgiveness...

What a different world we're in, when we love without conditions.

Loving absolutely everyone means only that we have forgiven them, and ourselves, for being 'only human'.

Once this begins, people are such beautiful beings who react well to acts of kindness and respect.

It becomes a bit like a club, where love is the only hobby, and humor just follows along.

What is
Unconditional love?

It's a gift
From up above.

It causes us
To be real kind

To enemies
That we may find.

It's never saying,
"You, I hate."

Or, "Loving you,
I think can wait."

It's acting now.
It's being true.

You love them.
They love you.

Now, that wasn't
Very hard.

You weren't even
On your guard.

You will
Be drawn

To love
Some more.

I think
That's just

What hearts
Are for.

Unconditional
Love, I say,

I think there is
No better way.

I HAVE LEARNED
TO MAKE
A CONCIOUS
DECISION,

AND
RIDE IT
ALL THE WAY
THROUGH.

YET,
I RESERVE THE RIGHT
TO CHANGE
MY MIND...

YOU KNOW YOU ARE

GETTING OLD,

WHEN YOU TAKE

SO MUCH MORNING

MEDICATION

IT'S LIKE HAVING

BREAKFAST...

IF YOU DON'T
HAVE SOMETHING
GOOD
TO SAY ABOUT A
STUBOTSIO,
DON'T SAY ANYTHING
AT ALL!

STORE OWNER:

IT'S CLOSING TIME. I'M
AFRAID YOU'LL HAVE
TO LEAVE.

PATRON:

THAT'S OK.
I'VE BEEN THROWN
OUT OF
BETTER PLACES
THAN THIS!

Patricia A. Fisher

This Too Shall Pass

This world, where we come from, is quite a place. Just when I think I've written all I can, I am reminded of something else.

I have been on the receiving end of a lot of challenges. I find these challenges to be the way of the world.

Each day is a new day full of promises and dreams. Each day we must overcome difficulties. Yet, occasionally, a day can be like a big yummy cake in our own favorite flavor. There is also a topping on this cake.

I find that life's process is the cake, and the topping is that warm satisfaction when a challenge has been met.

Yes, life is a series of challenges. This may be why life seems so hard sometimes. It may be why some of us never get bored.

One of my greatest gifts is my knowing that life is only the decision of what to do while we wait. I hope to know all God's secrets, when I get to the end of the line. If I never find out, I hope I won't even care.

I guess good sleep is high on the list. It takes the magical, restorative, power of sleep to begin each new day, and each new challenge.

In the Autumn of my life, I have acquired ways to really enjoy what the world puts in front of me.

I've discovered that real people are much more enjoyable, and lovable, than any Super Human I may have created.

For the most part, I live with joy in my heart. Life can really be that big luscious cake...

This is because, I not only conquered huge challenges, but I had fun along the way.

This world needs a lot of love, and I just happen to enjoy the practice of loving.

Love sent my way is, hopefully, never wasted, and "Oh, how good it feels!"

Yes, I have made it through the many years… I have lived, both yin and yang, and everything in between. I am like tempered steel, or a pair of comfortable shoes. Actually, I am a part of all things, and my spirit is as if it's Christmas all year long.

My Heavenly Father appears to be using me as a vessel of light, and an instrument of Love, Respect, and Truth. My books are a vehicle for this purpose.

No, I am not perfect. I am perfectly imperfect! I'm just a limited person. Truth is my guide, and loving people is my joy.

People of Earth, I thank you for the support all along the way. Thank you for helping me see, and thank you for helping me feel again.

To my amazement, the older I get, the happier I am. Laughter is my good friend, and it is infectious.

I wish for every person to feel the happiness I feel, and when happiness seems just out of reach, this is only part of the process. More than likely, "This too shall pass..."

Oh Brother

Having only sisters, and no brothers all my life, makes me thankful for my brothers-in-law. (I prefer to call them, simply, "my brothers").

So, they never had sisters. Maybe, they enjoy having a couple of sisters-in-law!

My other Mother lived many years caring for four handsome men (her husband, Bob and their three sons, Dennis, Bill, and Tom).

I asked her how it was, living with four 'hunks' all those years. She said, "You just get use to it!"

Well, her husband, Bob, has passed away, and my other Mother is enjoying her life in an assisted living home. Their three sons are living here and there, and they have become kind and gentle men. They are not only beautiful on the outside, they are beautiful on the inside.

Imagine my joy, when this family came into my life and heart. We all seem to love each other, and I have been accepted, graciously into their lives.

I hope I never 'get use to' having brothers, as it would ruin part of the fun! Loving brothers is yet another kind of love...

Oh, brother...

The World Sucks

To quote Steve Henneman, my therapist: "Sometimes the world sucks, and I just have to wait until it passes."

I immediately internalized this, and made it my own. Since then, I have had no suicidal thoughts to speak of. That saying made me feel more like well-balanced people. I don't think many well-balanced people think of ending their lives very often.

Letting the world suck, and just waiting 'till it stops, makes me think that I'm coping the same way most everyone does.

I don't usually say anything sucks. Yet, no other phrase or sentence could have erased the terrible urges to end my life.

I found that a meaningful connection, with my fellow Earthlings, is far less lonely, and less frightening, than that hellish place I use to endure.

Sharing difficulties, with others, makes more sense than being in hell all by myself, and I have no idea, where people go, when they die at their own hand.

The bible says, "Thou shalt not kill." I guess, this means even yourself...

Sometimes, when I am looking for loopholes, something from the bible pops into my head. I use that information for much needed guidance...

When I joined my fellow man, I found more than a connection during hard times. I found the joy of equality, a sense of belonging, more love, and life became a lot more fun! I am happily content a lot of the time, and I am grateful.

So, gentle reader, if you're not sure what there is to live for, read this account of what you might miss.

The choice I made was a good one for me.

Now "My cup runneth over" and
I can see what I never saw before
– even with my eyes closed...

God bless you gentle reader, and
thank you for your time.

Saying Goodbye

Saying goodbye is done in many different ways, probably as many ways as there are people.

Sometimes saying goodbye is sweet, when parting with a bill you have paid.

It is sweet leaving a room where people have invited you into their argument.

Leaving is sweet, when your husband and his mother are sorting tons of pictures of people you've never met...

It feels so good to bid farewell to your dentist after a root canal.

Yet, seriously, farewell can be sweet, when a loved one passes away, and you both had a chance to talk over old times.

Goodbye is sweet when your pet has to be put down and it passes away in your arms.

People from way back have tried to express parting from someone or something they care about.

For example:

"Parting is such sweet sorrow..."

By William Shakespeare

"The heart knows not its own depth until the hour of separation."

By Kahlil Gibran

A two-year-old simply cries and shouts "No!" when it's time to leave all the fun at bedtime.

I for example, detested going to bed "because I was so afraid I would miss out on something."

Ya know? A simple "See ya later" takes the sting out of Goodbye. Goodbye sounds so final where "See ya later" gives promise to a new day.

"See ya later not only takes the sting out of 'goodbye' but invites us to look forward to seeing each other again...

People tend to say "Let's get together sometime!" The answer is usually "Ya, that sounds like fun!"

After a lot of years and many times of putting off making arrangements, I thought, "There must be a better way!" Then an idea bubbled up in my head. The next time "Let's get together sometime!" came about, I said "When?"

Since then we don't waste our time getting caught up in something and never seeing our friends...

There are indeed, many ways to say "Goodbye" but for me not saying it at all is the best!

Book of Rules

A Handbook for Friendship

If I had
A handbook for friendship,

I'd know
Just what to do.

I'd know
Just what to say,

When passing time
With you.

I'd know
Just when to speak.

I'd know
All dos and don'ts.

I'd know
All shoulds and shouldn't.

I'd know
All wills and won'ts.

If I had
A book of rules

'Bout how
To get along,

There'd be
No room for fighting.

Our friendship
Would be strong.

I'd know
Just when to care.

Forever,
I would know

Not to
Hurt your feelings.

We'd be
More friend than foe...

We had
A disagreement.

I threw you
Out of my heart!

Oh, but no,
Not really!

I don't
Want us to part!

The earth
Still has its limits.

So
It seems to me.

We just
Can't be perfect

In friendship.
Don't you see?

We cannot read
Each other's minds,

Or know
Just what to do.

When each one
Needs the other,

How can we both
Be true?

We are not
The only ones

To fail
Once in a while.

Everyone
Has trouble.

So,
Let us wear a smile...

All I say
Is what I know

From living
All this time.

So, maybe
If we talk a bit,

(You add
Your thoughts to mine).

I will start
By asking you

If you need
My aid.

Then, if you
Will tell me true,

My friend,
We'll have it made!

We are
So very different.

What would be
The use?

If we both
Were just the same,

The same words
We would choose.

If we find
We don't agree,

Very much
At all,

If we fight
So miserably,

And
Joy is very small,

If we cannot
Find some peace,

And happiness
As friends,

It appears
That we must part,

If our heart
Never mends.

We could love
Heart to heart,

And, maybe
Soul to soul.

Each other, we,
Just would not see,

If fighting
Is our goal.

What do you think,
My dear friend?

I've spoken
All I can.

Is our friendship
Worth it?

Is it
Something grand?

I could
Ask you questions –

Not jumping
In your space.

I could share
My thoughts 'bout me,

And this
Would change the pace.

Then you'd feel
Less on the spot.

Your story,
You could tell.

Let your best
Be for your friend.

Their best to you
As well.

If I had
A handbook,

With how
To get along,

We'd have
All the answers.

Our lives
Would be a song.

If we had
The answers,

From that old
Book of rules,

We'd be wise
Together,

Not lonely
Being fools...

Patricia A. Fisher

Don’t ‘Wanna’ Go Home

Why do we
Have to go home,

When you and I
‘Wanna’ go roam?

There are more
Places to see.

So many more
Places to be.

There are some
Places we’ve been.

We ‘wanna’ leave,
And go there again.

We've been gone
Almost half the year.

Now, we must
Go home, my dear.

He tells me
That he's feelin' low.

He still says
He has places to go.

I tell him
"Let us be thankful."

He tells me,
"Let's get a tank full."

There is a place
That we really like –

A place where we
Like to go hike.

Way far out
In the desert we go –

Both of us
Are walking real slow.

Then, in time,
We pick up the pace,

Then, we wander
All over the place.

We never are
Bored about it.

No, in Fact,
We don't want to quit.

I tell him,
"Ok, we will go.

We have no money,
I want you to know."

"This has never
Stopped us before,

Though, we have
Our payments galore!"

He looks at me,
With big brown eyes.

Responsibility
Suddenly dies.

I feel myself
Start to give in.

The devil thinks
He's going to win!

'My' Dennis, now,
Is truly possessed.

His wanderlust
Won't let him rest.

On our travels,
He is now hooked.

I look at him,
And say, "We are cooked!"

I try once more,
"It's me or the street!"

He says to me,
"I'll miss you, my sweet!"

All of a sudden
I finally find,

My love, we're not
In that much of a bind..."

The Favor I Owe the World

Fittingly, it was Halloween night. Sleep did not come easy, because I was suffering from a physical difficulty.

I awoke at 8AM, and was doing ok, except for residual pains in my body.

Then, I made the mistake of returning to bed. A lot of times, doing this gives me nightmares. I awakened with pain in my joints, and this time, pain in my stomach. I felt as if I had been beaten, and, for a long period of time, didn't know if I would recover...

I dragged myself down the stairs, and pushed the button to start some 'life renewing coffee'.

My physician has warned me about coffee and several other delights. It appears that most of my indulgences are no longer tolerated by my body.

Yet, if I don't partake of them, I find my difficulties too heavy to bare.

Coffee is a double edge sword for me. It seems to usher me out of bad dreams, and into a brand new day. Yet, physically, it is abominable.

At 56 years of age, I find a different array of challenges.

The things that have 'brought me through' in the past, are a detriment to my body now.

Giving up gracefully, the things of youth, means giving up almost everything digestible. It means giving up agility, as the body begins to deteriorate. Arthritis seems to catch hold, at a certain age, and walking becomes more difficult.

Everything taken for granted by youth, becomes more dear as time goes by. A person becomes more thankful for any capability, and begins to see what's really important: A smile, a kind word, a bit of respect, and, occasionally, a helping hand.

A person might wonder why I
think I owe the world a favor,
while I'm living with signs of old age
and mental illness.

Through it all, I have been
supported by people, quite
possibly, in as much need as I.

I took on the role of a person with
huge difficulties. I grasped onto
people, who chose to live a life of
service, and I have really
appreciated this gift.

So, I find myself indebted to these
'angels on Earth', and I choose to
share all of my secrets.
I hope that, in the sharing of
these, I might give strength to my
fellow man – including those
who may have assisted me in the
past.

EARTH

I want to share my truth, that I am surprised to even be alive, and that my life has been an amazing journey.

I wouldn't change a thing, as every experience has brought me to where I am.

Yes, I am indebted to all the people who believed in me – even when I could not believe in myself.

I am told I am mentally challenged, and each day I am ready to fight the fight. Yet, the fight is laced with memories of the good.

Thankfully, I live this life, loving and being loved.

I live this life, with all its challenges and promises, and there have been a few broken dreams.

As for nightmares, I guess the devil may be nipping at my heels.

I choose to accept what I cannot change, and I choose to live on with both the good and the not so good.

Earth is definitely an amazing ride, and, at least I know I am not alone...

For this and more, I want to give back,

The Favor I Owe the World...

Intro to Where Does It Hurt

This next piece is dedicated to 'Sweet Mary' and her daughter, Alex.

I don't know 'Little Alex', but if she is anything like her Mother, she is just beautiful, inside and out!

Turn the page, and read about a mother's love. This piece is entitled, "Where Does It Hurt"?

YOU
ARE
THE
JOY

Where Does It Hurt

Where does it hurt,
    My little one?
Does it need a kiss?

You are the joy
    Of my life.
With that, how can you miss?

You're too young
    To talk to me.
Your smile is like a jewel.

You are very
    Valuable –
Even when you drool...

Your smile is so
    Infectious.
From your sweet face to mine.

Strained plums and peas
    And carrots,
On yummy food you dine.

You are mine
    Forever –
Not only 'till 18.

That will happen
    Very soon,
And I will be waiting.

I had best not
    Look away –
Not even for a bit.

Parents over
    Centuries
Have spoken about it.

You babes grow up
    So very fast,
Before our very eyes.

When old you get,
    You may admit,
We are so very wise!

Little baby
    You don't know
The value of a dollar...

You don't know
    'Bout finances.
But you know how to holler!

It all starts
    A lot like this,
"My babe, you are the boss.

When you get mad,
    And out of sorts,
Your bottle, you may toss.

Your little lungs
    Get lots of use,
When there's something you
     Need.

As you grow,
    We all know
You'll grow just like a weed.

At two years old
    You learn to shout,
NO! NO! NO!

Before I even
    Say a word,
You begin to grow!

You'll get real long
    And lanky
Around the age of seven.

You'll then fill out,
    And change again,
So sweet, a gift from heaven.

Then you'll meet
    A someone,
And you may start to feel

Hormones
    In your body.
Your torment gets more real.

As a teen,
    You will appear,
Crazy as a loon!

Life just won't
    Seem right to you.
So, don't grow up too soon.

If this goes
    Agreeably,
You'll meet someone to love.

Maybe you'll
    Get married,
In front of God above.

Then you may
    Have a child
Just the same as you.

You will gasp,
    As I did,
"Oh God, what shall I do?"

You'll tell your babe,
    "Where does it hurt?
Does it need a kiss?

You are the joy
    Of my life.
With that, how can you miss?"

Panic Attack

This AM I went to the lab for
some tests.

Last night, I had a panic attack,
and I was afraid of seeing more
spiders that weren't there...

I had taken a sleeping pill, and
the side effects frightened me
greatly!

I controlled my impulses to react,
and forced myself to fall asleep.

This AM, at the lab, I was having
my blood drawn, when a lab tech
really screwed up!

She inserted a large needle, into my left arm, while ignoring my requests for the smaller, butterfly needle... After not reaching a vein, she started moving the needle around under my skin. She didn't seem to hear my protests.

I told her she was scaring me, and that she must have hit a tendon.

Ignorant of my fear, she changed to my right arm. The same thing happened again, as she moved the needle around under my skin.

I became angry and afraid. Just then, a tech named Dave walked over. I began to cry...

He drew my blood in a couple of seconds, and said I was an easy draw (blood test talk).

Dave always finds my veins easily, and asked that I request him Monday through Thursday.

I reported Keesha for not having enough experience, and for not really caring about what she was doing.

As I left the building, I had another panic attack. I was hysterical for quite awhile, even with 'my' Dennis at my side.

I just knew that Super Humans had come back. This Keesha person had all of them agreeing with her unprofessional attitude and unethical technique.

Hence, I thought that Keesha was hurting me – backed by a powerful force of hundreds of Super Humans.

I didn't want to live, if these people were running my life by hurting me.

Instead of expounding on the subject of suicide, I immediately called my therapist, Steve.

He helped me pull myself together, and we made a plan for the rest of the day. I took an Ativan for the anxiety, and as I write, I am willing to believe again, that I may be mentally challenged.

Keesha was maybe one single person, who just didn't seem to care. Maybe she was prejudice, which is very, very sad...

Strength went out of my body, again, and as usual, I must lie down for a power rest.

I will report back to Steve, and once this is done, I can go on with my life.

I give thanks to 'my' Dennis, my therapist Steve, and Aurora Community Mental Health Center.

I could not go on without them!

Smooch!!

For 'My' Dennis

I wish I had
Some way to thank you.

I wish I had
Something to say.

I've something
To tell you – about you,

Something about
Everyday...

Everyday
That you love me,

Those are the days
I am blessed

There's no one else
In the world dear.

I chose you
'Cause you are the best.

Every time
That I'm with you,

My darling,
You light up my life.

I know
From much time together.

I'm happy
That I am your wife.

There's never really
A plain day,

Because
You make my heart sing.

32 years
Together,

31 wearing
Your ring.

I never get
Tired of you.

Maybe, that's just
'Cause of love.

I will be
With you forever.

Is forever
Even enough?

Thank you
For all your support dear.

You're good about that
Everyday.

Thank you
For all of your humor,

And loving me
All of the way.

Let me sing
Your praises.

I am
A lucky girl!

There isn't
Anyone like you.

No, not in all
Of the world...

Ouch!
Ow!
Ow!

Mine is Worse

When Mom was upset, she'd say, "Wait 'till you get my age! Then you'll know what trouble is! When you get my age, you'll find out toilet paper costs money! You're only 15. What troubles could you have?"

The message was really, "Mine is worse".

As a lot of you know, I grew up thinking that my Mom was going to die. When someone would give me a choice about something, I would think,
"What would be best for Mom?"

I was so bombarded by hearing,
"Mine is worse" that I
automatically put my feelings,
needs and choices last...
Then I put Mom's first...

As time went on, I put everyone's
first! I would choose what I
thought *they* would like, not what
I would like.

I would make these decisions
automatically, and didn't know I
was doing it.

People don't ask you what you
would like, in order to hear their
heads rattle! They choose to give
you the choice as a gift.

By constantly being told "Mine is worse" I became invisible. I didn't matter. My problems were never worse than anyone else's, and I wasn't allowed to have my feelings.

I concentrated on rescuing others, as if they were broken, and neglected myself.

From now on:

I will not think everyone has it worse than I.

I will not feel that I am less valid, because their needs are greater.

I will not continue making
decisions by what another
person wants.

I will let people give me the gift of
choice, and I will accept their
honoring me...

I have learned that nobody knows
who has it worse. It just
cannot be measured...

Isn't That Funny

Ever since I was very, very young, humor has taken me through it all.

Discomfort was so difficult for me! Maybe reality was just too heavy to bear. So I blocked it all out with humorous smart cracks.

I don't remember having or showing my feelings, until age 19, when I first started therapy. I must have divulged a million secrets, and I must have cried at least as many tears.

I must have thought that everyone was more rigid and desperate than I. I ran around helping people, when I didn't really have anything to give...
I was a good little helper. After all, my Mama always said so.

I was very popular in school. I guess my classmates didn't know how empty I was in my heart.

Jokes broke the spell of any subject that made me feel. I was so afraid of letting the world inside.

When I did listen, I was in control. I directed the conversation, and I asked the questions. I was a good listener.

These days, after 37 years of therapy, I still have my sense of humor. I can laugh at things that use to hurt me. The difference is that I replaced the desperation with true happiness.

I have been unconditionally loved by people who knew how. I have found guidance, and people have listened to me open mindedly, without judgment.

They have helped me find my own answers, and some have marveled at how I can laugh at the devil.

Laughter has come to me in the midst of a troubled mind. I've known, since an early age, the joy and relief of hearing people's laughter.

These days, I am not empty, and my humor is not designed to keep people away.

Today, I have choices, and I am pliant – not rigid.

Sometimes there are still panic attacks that threaten to devastate me, but most of the time, I am content.

Laughter now connects me with people to love, and I am finally secure enough to help others.

The Last Three Days

My stress began around 30 days ago. Finally, it reached a peak, and I prayed very hard that I would survive!

Something significant was happening on each of the last 3 days:

- The first meeting about my publishing company changing to non-profit November 16th.

- Our 31st wedding anniversary November 17th.

.

- The third anniversary of my Mom's death November 18th.

At first, I hardly noticed the symptoms. They began slowly, and were fairly unremarkable.

Then, my sleep became less restful. One early morning, I saw some large spiders that weren't really there. Sometimes, I woke up crying, and one night I woke up screaming!

All these fears had been gathering in the back of my mind. Finally, they had to surface...

I put myself back on sleeping pills, and this is part of what saved me.

On two of the special days, Dennis and I argued more than ever! I reacted ten times worse than the situation called for, and by this time, I was in unbearable symptoms!

My temper grew into rage, and I couldn't verbalize enough obscenities! It was awful for Dennis and me...

Dear Gentle Reader, maybe you can relate to these horrible feelings, and the occasional arguments that do not seem to end.

Craziness accompanied my anger, and I did not know what was real. I took personally small indiscretions by other people. They appeared to be directed only to me, and, of course, they were backed by that huge force I call Super Humans.

I called emergency, and was given the option of going to the hospital. The person I spoke to was so very kind and compassionate. She was another reason I made it through...

I have told you, gentle reader. My physical strength goes away at these upsetting times. That is why I ended up sleeping for 18 hours today.

I am hoping to be able to leave the house tomorrow – without getting the awful messages of rage and unreality.

My Dear Reader, I share this story with you and I want you to know that I do live through hell. I also fight my way back!

I want you to know that I love planet Earth, its inhabitants and I revere my place in the order of things.

Suicide is still no longer an option for me and I live with love in my heart.

Yes I remain a warrior, and many times humor is by my side.

As often as possible, I make up dumb jokes.

My Dennis has told me, "If you go to heaven before I do, I will remember your laughter the most."

Isn't that worth all the effort of living through *The Last Three Days?*

Coffee Beans And Pomegranates

My heart is dancing in the middle of cleaning the house! Endorphins are high and the feeling is good.

I've just spoken with my sister Kate. She's coming here early to help with Thanksgiving dinner. Mom use to help but she's been gone 3 years now...

Kate's husband, Bob, is a good guy. He never says a bad thing about or to anyone. He seems to take life in his stride, and we like him a lot.

Dennis will be here. He carves the turkey. He carves it with an electric knife we got from his cousin.

My favorite part is, of course, the love. Next in line, is seeing the turkey come out of the oven. It's all golden brown and it smells just wonderful! I usually snitch the first delectable bites while it is being carved.

At this point, there are so many last minute things to do. Gravy is one and for our bunch, we need about a gallon! Also there is fresh homemade bread right from the oven… m-m-m-m-m!

We manage to serve the same Waldorf salad that Mom did all those years…

Speaking of Mom, we're going to miss her again this year. For a lot of years, she fixed Thanksgiving dinner. She always tried to feed everybody, not only on holidays, but all of the time! Mothers are like that...

In later years – even when she could hardly walk – she would always make me a cup of her good coffee.

I gripe about Mom sometimes, but I know in my heart, she was a good person.

Daddy died long before Mom did. He loved Christmas, I think, because he enjoyed giving gifts.

I just know that Mom and Dad are up in heaven dancing.

The list of people we have lost is long. Sister Jan, and brother-in-law Denny, are sorely missed… They were good people, and I pray that they are not in pain. I ask that they have laughter, because they cried too many tears here on Earth.

We mustn't forget our little sister Wanda, who passed away about 50 years ago. She was with us for 8 short weeks, but she was never forgotten…

We have more nieces and nephews, but they appear to need their own space. We tend to let them be, and we are here if they ever change their minds.

It's holiday time, and I am tickled even to clean the house!

Kate is coming, and maybe Joan…

There will be good things to eat and drink, and the dining table will be decorated. The house is festive, and Kate is bringing *Coffee Beans and Pomegranates.*

Her daughter, Tanya, will be loved and cherished, though she will be miles away…

My heart is smiling. Maybe Nick will be here. He always has the most wonderful hugs!

Last, but not least, 'my' Dennis will be by my side. Our abundance is overflowing, and we give thanks for it all!

From this day forward, I will remember the holidays, as a perfect time for *Coffee Beans and Pomegranates…*

Today, I Have a Choice

Insanity is a funny thing – maybe not funny – maybe just a terrible thing…

I call my therapist to ask for help. I tell him everything that I am thinking. I tell him all my fears.

Sometimes I go 'under'. I drown in the 'mess' my thoughts have created.

Steve, my therapist, tries to tell me my thoughts are not true, and I cry…

The rug has been pulled out from under me for the millionth time. I am afraid, as if it was happening for the very first time, and I cry...

Recently, I crashed almost every day for over a week. I was so tired! Sleep came easy, but it was a fitful sleep.

You see, I had another breakdown a couple of weeks ago. I am still reeling from it.

When the bad ones are over, it's like being on a roller coaster ride. I go up, then down, again and again, until it finally stops.

Again, I call Steve. We talk, and then, after a while, I realize what is happening. This is the aftermath of another bad breakdown. It has happened many times before, and it will pass.

There have been times, when I could not stay out here in the world. I have had to be hospitalized. At these times, I have had no choice.

Steve asks me questions, hoping we will find answers, hoping to stop the insanity.

After that call, I sleep for 18 hours. I awaken, and the insanity breaks like a bad fever.

It appears that I have made it through again, without being locked away.

My Dennis has stayed alert and vigilant. He has been through this with me many times. Yet he worries as if it was his first time also.

Again, I call Steve... He has seen me through another bad one, as I have called him nearly 10 times.

Do I need the hospital? Do I have a choice?

I am suddenly hopeful. I am proud, like a warrior after a great battle. I look over my shoulder, and exclaim, "Wow! What was that?"

Then I look forward. I stand tall, because I have won another war. I whisper to myself that I don't need to be locked up. I don't have to walk down those halls, and cry in those rooms.

I've been very brave, and this makes me both tired and glad. I embrace my freedom for awhile, because I know,

"Today, I Have a Choice."

Just In Case

Just in case
My meds work,

I take them
Every day.

"Just in case
They help me,"

Is what
I always say.

They may just
Solve my problems

With what comes
To my mind.

My doctors
Always ask me,

When I am
In a bind,

"Do you take
Your meds, dear,

Because we see
Your pain?

It helps you
Think more clearly,

When it gets to
Your brain."

I tell them
Yes, I take it,

Just in case
It works.

It may just help
That part of me –

That part of me
That hurts.

My mental health
Professionals

Are totally
Surprised!

I do
What they tell me.

They are so
Very wise.

I'm told to trust
Professionals

Hired for
My health.

I feel they're
More important

Than monetary
Wealth.

I just cannot
Do everything

The doctors
Say to me.

Yes, it seems
Impossible,

Though I pay
A fee.

So, I do
Everything I can

To try
And get along.

I just do
The best I can.

Now, how can that
Be wrong?

The taking of
My medicine

Is where
I stay more true.

Just in case
It helps me,

It's something
I can do…

WHEN YOU LET

SOMEONE MAKE YOU

ANGRY,

THEY ARE IN

CONTROL OF YOU...

A BAD DAY

DOESN'T HAVE TO BE

ALL BAD.

IT CAN BE

A BAD HALF A DAY,

AN HOUR,

OR EVEN A MOMENT.

TWO SOCKS WERE SITTING IN THE DRYER.

ONE SOCK SAID TO THE OTHER,

"LOOK AT ALL THESE HOLES. WELL, I'LL BE DARNED!"

CAN A PERSON

REALLY BE HUMBLE,

WHILE THEY ARE

SITTING THERE

TELLING YOU

HOW HUMBLE

THEY ARE?

Of Wine and Roses

Maybe some people learned how to drink properly. I did not. My drinking days are thankfully gone, and so are the wine and the roses.

In the past, I could do very little without alcohol (Fix dinner, Put on makeup, or Dine out).

I use to have a couple of drinks before dinner. When we went out, I had them even when Dennis didn't. He would sit there and wait for me to finish.
Then we would eat.

He use to tell me that I wasn't myself when I drank.

I just thought that, since he rarely drank, he just didn't understand.

His parents never had alcohol in their house, and mine did. I decided my decision was mine, and his was his.

As I look back, most of my family's difficulties were medicated with liquor. I was no acceptation.

In 1990, I got into trouble. I was caught driving while impaired.

They took my driver's license away for 3 months.

I did some community service, and I paid extra for my car insurance 3 years in a row.

The court also ordered me to go to some hard core meetings about drinking.

I sat there among the domestically violent, a pedophile, people who physically attacked others, and other people who changed
when they drank.

I was just as troubled. I could have hit someone with my car. I could have crippled or killed someone.

Christmas day, of that year, I had a wine cooler. It was my least favorite drink, because it had a lot of sugar in it. I always thought that more sugar meant less alcohol. So, I usually chose dry wine or plain hard liquor.

I recommend a wine cooler if you want to quit drinking. There is nothing worse…

So, I had one wine cooler, and I didn't like how I felt. I finally discovered that drinking alcohol was like living my life with a monkey on my back.

So, I quit! I quit right there on Christmas day!

Now, if I stutter or trip over something, we all know it isn't the booze...

When I first quit drinking, I marveled at what I could do without a drink in my hand.

I'd run to Dennis, and report all my successes. I'd say to him, "Dennis, I cleaned the kitchen without drinking! Dennis, I made dinner without a drink! Dennis, I don't need a drink to have a conversation with people we meet!"

I use to embarrass myself, by not knowing what I did. Then, I'd find out later what a fool I was.

Saving money is part of my satisfaction. We now spend about one third less, when we go out for dinner. We spend less at home, because we no longer have hard liquor in the house.

I went to a couple of A.A. meetings, and came away with a couple of sayings that have helped me over the years:

(1.) Principles over personalities (Accomplish your goal, even if people involved affect you adversely.)

(2.) Immediately make amends, for anything you may have said or done, to hurt another person.

This Christmas day I will be a non-drinker for 13 years. It's been about that long since I've been to an A.A. meeting.

This may sound odd, but my cravings for booze, did not stay real strong. At times, I would like a glass of wine, but a sip is all I take. I don't remember even one sip this last 12 months.

There is always wine in our wine rack, but I never think of it as being there for me. I guess I could say, "I just don't need it, and the freedom feels good!"

The good old days are happening
right now, and I don't need the
wine or the roses.

I prefer the more sturdy flowers,
like the happy faces of Daisies,
and a well-chilled,
un-aged, bottle
of H_2O.

Goodbye, Super Humans.

I don’t need you anymore.

You make me crash down to the
floor.

You cause me anger, pain, and
shame.

I don’t want to play your game.

You send me messages through
the air.

You want control. It isn’t fair!

You cause me pain, and make me
pay!

I command you, “Go away!”

I have an idea that will help me overcome the power of the Super Humans. It involves reality, and reality is less confusing than my 'Super Human world.'

In reality, we are all in the same boat. We must all keep trying or perish, and we can't read each other's minds.

We shed tears, when we feel vulnerable, and this is a miracle, if we don't have to cry all the time...

The reality is that most of us want the kind of love that makes us feel less alone. We also have hope this will bring us joy.

When one of us is in peril, others come to our aid. We are a society that cares for the individual, and we, the people, care about each other.

When we can, we share our happiness, instead of one person trying to steal it from the other.

We need to take care of ourselves, so we will have health and energy, to embrace life to its fullest.

Our lives are very dear to us, and sometimes, we feel like hiding! Fear has touched every one of us, which only makes life more valuable. At least, we are not alone...

We have many feelings – including confusion. Sometimes, that's all we know is that we are confused.

Yet, we forge ahead, trying not to take ourselves too seriously. We try not to take everything so personally, and we search for peace of mind.

Challenge appears to keep us interested and we try so very hard...

We know we are not perfect. Yet, some of us aspire to be, and some of us settle for being 'perfectly imperfect.'

It still remains that in the real world we can be equal. No one is really better than anyone. Nor is anyone at all less than another.

When we are slaves to an unclear power our demons run rampant! We have unbelievable fear, and rage takes over our lives! We fight an unclear enemy, and we are more lost, and bewildered, than if we were fighting in a real war between countries. We must eternally guess what the message really is. We cry a million tears, and get a reputation for having a temper.

I'll take reality. That's where you ask, when you don't understand. That is where you are actually told in words what you need to know. When you hurt, you have a viable reason. When you smile, it comes from your heart.

When you lose someone, you gather together, and mourn. Whatever the feeling, there is usually a very real reason why it is there.

As I say goodbye to my enemy, the Super Humans, it is with trepidation. They have been with me for 37 years.

I feel they have molded me, and they have shared a very private and personal part of my life and body. To my surprise, it has not been all bad.

As I write, I say goodbye with a sweet sadness. But I will not miss the outrage and anger of that excruciating, emotional pain.

I've learned many things, but I don't know what I learned directly from them, if anything...

I wrote this next goodbye poem before the rest of this piece. I must tell this power to leave me alone, but the anger feels quite odd...

"Don't you take my happiness!
What you want, I only guess!

You came to me and down I fell!
You brought me to the
depths of hell!

I don't think God lets this be –
Super Humans running free.

You're no longer welcome here.
Because my life is very dear.

Super Humans at my door,
I don't need you anymore..."

An ending
And
A beginning...

S
S
S
I don't NEED you ANYMORE!

Come On! You Can Do It!

Come On! You can do it!
I tell this to myself.
Old age is now upon me.
I worry 'bout my health.

A pain inside my shoulder,
The graying of my hair,
I walk a little wobbly.
Complaints, I have my share.

My face has lines and wrinkles.
My body weighs much more,
Than when I was a youngster.
Yes, I fight that war.

But, while all this is happening,
I will tell you true.

Though my body's aging,
My heart knows what to do.

I gaze upon a sunset,
Or watch a flower bloom.
I treasure one who loves me.
I listen to a tune.

Folks have said,
Oh, outer space,
I really
Must go there!

It would be
So wonderful
To see a place
So rare!"

They say they're bored
With where they live.
This Earth
Is not enough.

They want to go
To outer space,
So they can see
More stuff!

Well, let me see.
What can I say,
About this Earth
We're on?

I don't get bored
One little bit.
It's where
I do belong.

I have no wish
To go away,
Or see
Another place.

'Cause Earth is full
Of mystery,
As much as
Outer space.

I've said before,
"We're not plugged in
To get our body's
Power.

We walk and talk.
We laugh and cry.
Above all Earth
We tower.

Just watch
My little finger.
I'll show you
How it moves.

A miracle
All by themselves,
These fingers
That I use...

Yes, Earth is full
Of mystery.
I hope you
Understand.

For we can see
A miracle
By looking
At our hand...

Something Very Glorious
Our Dearest Cynthia

There's something very glorious
'Bout helping just one soul.
Helping in the millions
Really is my goal.

Yet, when I reached
A single being,
It was
Oh so great!

I'm so glad
That I could help
Before it was
Too late.

I was so thrilled
To hear the news!
My heart was
Full of glee,

Just because
You're letting go
Of fear
That use to be.

Welcome dear,
To planet Earth,
And also to
My heart,

Because you try
So desperately
Just to do
Your part.

In this world
We must be brave,
And meet our fear
Straight on.

Congratulations
My sweet love.
Some of your fear
Is gone!

My advice to you
Would be
To try and tell
The truth.

Respect and love
Each one you meet,
And this will be
The proof,

That you are on
A rocky road,
Working
Very hard,

To be among
Us human beings,
Who seem to be
On guard.

If you try
And try again
To love
Just everyone,

If you give
Love to yourself,
The world
Becomes more fun!

Welcome
My sweet gentle soul.
Let love be
Your only goal.

More and more
You will be free.
For I can feel you
Loving me...

Eyes of Green

There's a comfort level
That I must find.

I'm having feelings
Of every kind.

I just don't want
To lose my mind.

The wheels move slowly,
When they grind.

I am caught
In the web of life.

I am wounded,
As if by a knife.

Though there's pain
It cannot be seen,

Except within
My eyes of green.

I fight a war
That makes me frown.

Tears might come!
I fear I'll drown!

No matter how hard
I try to see,

I'm blinded by
Confusion in me...

So, here I am
With pen in hand,

I'm trying hard
To understand.

Was life for me
Ever clear?

Was contentment
Ever near?

Not quite at
The gates of hell,

But I'm not feeling
Very well...

The pain I'm in
Cannot be seen –

Except in sad old
Eyes of green.

Blessed are those
Who cannot speak

Blessed are they
Both timid and meek.

I am a person
Who knows many words.

Yet, I can't explain
How to sooth where it hurts.

My pain is subdued.
Yet, I still feel.

My comfort level
Just isn't real.

For I'm in a place
That I've never been –

Not quite familiar,
This place that I'm in.

That is the story
Of reasons why

I almost,
But didn't cry...

The Fam'

I wonder who
Makes your heart sing.

Who shares with you
Most everything?

Who knows just
What makes you tick?

Who loves you
Through thin and thick?

Whose big hugs
Are so complete?

For whom do you cook
So they can eat?

With whom
Do you fight so openly?

Who opens up
Your eyes to see,

That you are the one
Who makes them smile,

Though you don't visit
For awhile...

There's no one in
The world you see,

Whose love is true
Like family.

So I will stay
Just where I am,

So I can be
Close to my fam'...

My Man

My man is gone.
My body sighs.
Tears are gathering
'Neath my eyes.

Never again
To touch his hand,
I think about
My wedding band,

And how we were
Forever bound,
To be together,
With love we found.

Then, as if,
Mysteriously,
A tear falls down,
And then breaks free.

Another follows,
And then it falls,
While I'm studying
These four walls...

I look around
At things we shared,
And then I remembered
How much we cared.

He let me say,
"I love you."
How many times,
I never knew.

He would always
Say back to me,
"I love you, too."
That's how it would be.

I loved him so much!
I'd never know,
Who reached for whom,
When off we'd go.

Another tear
Fell onto the bed.
I don't even know
How many I shed.

When I was finished,
With tears from the loss,
I wanted to see him,
Whatever the cost.

I dried my eyes,
And remembered that he,
Had gone to the mountains
Only to ski...

The Warrior Patricia Anne

Dear Mr. Henneman,
May I be brief?
I had a good evening.
What a relief!

Our wonderful contact
Over the phone,
Gave me some power
To call my own.

Just a few minutes,
I want to say,
Gave me a workable
Day today!

Sometimes I think
That I ask a lot.
I talk to you,
Then, I think not.

I always want
To give thanks to you,
But, maybe thanks isn't
What I should do.

Maybe, if I
Had more good days,
Maybe, if I
Improved more ways,

Maybe, success
With having fun,
Would be like thanks,
When it's all done.

You work hard
At helping me.
When I'm upset,
You help me be...

I am so thankful
You're around,
But I must use
The ways I've found,

To help me cope
With Mother Earth.
I must find
What those are worth.

If you're just
A human being,
And you're not
An unreal thing,

If you're limited
Just like me,
You can't always
Help me be.

COUNCELOR
STEVE
WARRIOR
PATRICIA ANNE

If we're equal
At being strong,
Some of my calls
May be wrong.

Instead of saying,
"I thank you."
There could be more
I could do...

25 tools
To live my life,
Tools to help
With pain and strife,

Can all be found
In a book I wrote.
It's just me
This book will quote.

I will try
Hard as I can.
For I'm the warrior,
Patricia Anne...

Songs of the Bee Gee's

When I think of all the music in the world, I feel like my heart might burst!

Music, from the mouths of these men, has melted my armor and brought me to my knees! My tears fall, because I cannot fathom their greatness. I don't know how they can transfer me to this beautiful place of spirit and feeling...

I go to my pen, where God sometimes resides, and feebly begin to write...

As my words fall onto the pages, I find that there are no words to define this uplift of body, mind, and spirit. There are no words to tell how it feels, when the three of these are in sync, and I am soaring like an eagle on its way to God...

So, I let myself be filled to the brim with feelings I cannot explain. Though I am exaulted, I let my tears fall.

Again and again, I am in total awe, of the Bee Gee's, my fellow human beings...

We miss you, Mo'...

My Illness

I can make it
Without you!

I'm fine
All by myself!

There is something
About you

That's no good
For my health!

You want to have
Control of me –

Even against
My will.

There's one way
I can stop you.

I'll take a
Tiny pill.

When you control
My actions,

It takes me
Way far down.

I feel that you
Have reigns on me,

And I am
Hellward bound.

There's so much
Awful pain here –

A total lack
Of God.

I'm in the land
Of lies here.

What I think
Is quite odd...

I get to thinking
The devil is boss

Of the whole damn
Universe!

Love and goodness
And mercy

Just roll away
In a hearse!

I lie here with
Deadly poison

Coming out
In my speech.

I witness that all my
Good feelings

Are lost
And no longer in reach.

I am in
So much pain!

I don't know
What to do!

The strength
Is leaving my body,

But this isn't
Something new.

Then, I remember
That tiny pill

That changes
How I am.

Once it's in
My body,

I begin to
Give a damn...

It Feels So Good When It Stops

I look back over my shoulder, and
exclaim, "What was that?"
Sometimes, I don't know how far
out I've gone 'till it's over.
I don't even know how strong the
pain was until it is no longer
there.

Human resilience keeps me
amazed. How do people go
through outrageous battles with
their health, and fight their way
back strong enough to enjoy
what's left of their lives?

What is this driving force that keeps us not only wanting to survive, but maybe wanting to enjoy our lives again?

If we could bottle this force, we could make zillions, but the challenge, that is life, would no longer be there...

I cry, curse and expound on how I suffer. I fight life's battles, and write about many of them. As a writer and poet, I fill many hours with trying to put life into words.

Would I do this, if all I had to do was drink a bottle of this mysterious force?

I'm kind of proud of how I can get up every morning, and greet the day. I feel pretty great about winning my wars and sharing how I manage my difficulties. I think about someone I've helped, or some way I have made the world a better place, and a smile comes onto my lips.
My heart rises in my chest, and sometimes chills go through my body.

Could this be, if all we had to do was drink our motivation? I think not.

This world appears to be 'perfectly imperfect'.

It seems that there is just enough imperfection to bring about challenge, and enough promise of perfection to keep us interested.

This world could indeed be part of a great plan, and we are all invited to try and figure it all out. I don't think you could get that out of a bottle!

I am relieved, because I have just triumphed over another one of my great battles with mental illness. I can now smile again, and I can enjoy a world that I just finished cursing... All I can hope for at these times, is that It Feels So Good When It Stops!

Phew!
FEELS
GOOD!

ALL MY LIFE,

I HAVE TRIED TO GIVE

SO MUCH LOVE!

TODAY,

I FELT THE WORLD,

GIVE IT ALL BACK...

(February 11, 2005)

Low and Behold, & I'll Be Darned

Aurora Community Mental Health Center is more different than I thought. I've been going there for therapy since 1979.

I have been labeling the people who work there for all this time. As long as they were categorized, I felt somewhat safe... To me they were 'Super Humans', or 'The Other' or 'The S.H.s'. They were never just people...

The last few years, I have had no real comfort level.

A lot of times, I am in a state of unrest, and I blame my mental health professionals for causing this. I accuse them of controlling me, and for making me guess what they are planning for my case...

Low & behold & I'll be darned!
It finally came to me that they are just people... They are people who like me!

They care about me enough to keep me relatively safe, and they listen to me a lot!

Could it be that these professionals just keep caring, and I never knew it?

What a grand surprise, to all of a sudden, count so many who care about you!

All this time, I have thought that these people could see me in my home, no matter what I was doing, no matter what time it was, or how personal the moment.

I thought they could read my mind, and know what I was thinking. I had absolutely no privacy! It was as if I stood nude, and everyone else had their clothes on.

Low & behold, A.C.M.H.C. is a huge, non-profit company, just wanting to help people!

They just want to help! They went to school for it! They paid good money for school, just to help people!

This may seem like an easy no-brainer to you, but I've been working on this one for over 26 years...

God bless them all for the listening they do, for all the times they held their tempers, and for all the studying they did to get their certificates and degrees.

God bless every one of them for caring so very much that they devoted their entire lives to the betterment of us limited, but amazing, human beings.

THANKS...

'Becca'

Dear little 'Becca'
So sweet and small,

We send our love.
It's from us all.

We pray for you,
And your loving fam'.

I just can't say
How sad I am.

To a child
So full of love,

God is calling
From above.

He says that you
Will now have peace,

And all the pain
He says will cease.

For one so young
He knows that you

Have had your share
Of sadness too.

Dry your tears,
And look ahead.

To heavenly bliss
You will be led.

The angels will sing,
And they'll rejoice,

The moment they hear
Your childlike voice.

They'll invite you
To join in.

You'll be happier
Than you've been.

Heaven calls.
The time is right.

It's time that you
Give up the fight.

You've had much pain
For a little child.

It's time your grief
Was reconciled.

Then, sweet babe,
You will be free,

To run and play,
And well you'll be.

Wait for us,
When you get there.

For you must know
How much we care.

Little 'Becca' left us,
February 18, 2005.
She was 4 years old.

Lisa

Lisa is a person like none I've
ever met. I hesitate to write
about her, because I might fail to
capture her essence.

She is a mystery, and I haven't
known her very long. Yet, I have
witnessed her kindness, and a
wisdom beyond her 30 years.

I choose to trust the words of this
woman-child.

There is much I cannot see in her
mysterious face. She seems to
glide through her hours and days
being cheerful and kind.

What does she hide from this painful world, if not more pain? Her face stays alight with possibility and promise, and the world appears to belong only to her.

Yet, when I asked her for advice, her heart opened wide, and she shared her thoughts generously.

I have known her for only a brief moment in time, and I ask myself what is missing from her delightful presence...

My answer comes with ease, and I know that my heart can see her beauty, and in her beauty, I see nothing that is of a negative nature.

How on Earth has she managed to obtain these gifts, when she is only half my age?

This, my friends, is that mystery I spoke of, and I may never have an answer. For my world is changing, before my eyes, and I do not recognize a lot of what I see.

I see these amazing spirits, wearing human bodies. I have known of them for over half my life. They appear now and then, and they are incredible! They walk the Earth, with an uplifting quality. Their faces reflect a compassionate understanding of human life. Yet, they are mighty and strong.

I have been fortunate. For they have graced me with their presence many times. They give me hope for the human race, that we will not only live on, but we will flourish in truth, respect, and love.

I remember that I actually have met people like Lisa. In their goodness, I have seen them, like the beautiful loving spirits that they are.

Like Lisa, they glide through their hours and days, settling here and there like beautiful butterflies.

Places they've been are left better than they were before.

I said that I didn't know her, but as I write this piece, I discover that I do know Lisa after all...

Bite the Hand That Feeds Me

Do you have the energy
To help me like you do?

Do you talk about me?
Am I hard on you?

Where is it I stand?
Do I deserve respect?

Do I stand too close?
Is it me you would reject?

I use to be so sure
Of where it was I stood,

Of what respect I earned,
By doing what I could.

You don't ask of me
More than I can do.

I will do the same.
I care about you too.

Are we of equal strength?
I use to think that you

Were stronger than I was.
What was I to do?

Today, I have confusion
About what's truly real.

I can't make a decision,
Or go by what I feel.

Choices sometimes help me,
If I try real hard,

To stay with what is real,
Not being on my guard.

I choose to think we're equal,
That we have equal strength,

I choose to see your effort.
You'll go to any length,

To see that I'm ok,
That I am doing well.

I choose to see you caring,
But sometimes I can't tell,

If you're being honest,
If your words are true,

If your mannerisms
Show the real you.

Occasionally, when you respond,
I get a bit afraid.

My happiness just goes away.
My trust begins to fade.

If you were a person,
Without a grand degree,

We could talk 'bout this and that,
Without you changing me.

Please don't go on changing me,
Because I am ok.

Do not model who I'll be
Like you did today!

I guess I'm really angry,
Because we both can't be,

The person that he is,
And he cannot be me.

I'm finally understanding
That he has been well trained.

It doesn't mean he's smarter,
Or that he's better brained!

Both of us are equal.
There's nothing to conceal.

He can't be me. I can't be he,
And this is how I feel...

I Call It Love

My sisters and I got together at a gallery where they both had their art pieces displayed. We shared our thoughts about the pieces offered, and caught up on old times.

Mom would have been proud of the three of us. We related to each other, like well-balanced people, and showed love and respect toward each other.

I almost got a glimpse of Mom smiling down from Heaven. It was a short burst of appreciation, as she may have noticed that we were not only at peace with each other, but we were having a very good time!

Right before she died, Mom wished for the three of us to stay together. She wanted us to love each other long after her passing.

Since Mom's passing, I have not really felt her presence. It is as if she just disappeared into Heaven, and began a wonderful life there... She may be catching up with Daddy, and my sisters Wanda and Jan.

She could be reuniting with her beloved, biological Mom. The last time they saw each other was when Mom was in her late teens.

So, the three of us were left behind, with our various ways of relating to each other.

It appears that we have all become somewhat creative late in life.

We all have in common our own special way of contributing to the arts, and we have begun to share these things with each other.

No, it was not Christmas... Yet, we met with love in our hearts. At closing time, we stayed outside the gallery just talking, laughing, and loving. At the gallery, we were just three sisters doing our own thing.

Many years I have waited for a day like this. Many tears have been shed, and many prayers have been spoken, but God works at his own speed and in his own way...

At long last, I watch us, as we slowly gravitate toward each other. Our wounds have been healed, and our hearts are open wide.

We begin to share a part of life we only had glimpses of before.

I call this part family.
I call it friendship.
I call it love...

Ode to My Little Red Beetle

They say our stocks
Are lowering.

They're plummeting
To the ground.

Each time we get
Our stock report

We watch our funds
Go down.

Three thousand little dollars,
Then seven thousand more,

Go right down from the ceiling.
We watch them hit the floor...

They say we're not alone,
That others pay the price,

Because of all the people,
Who became a sacrifice.

On September eleven,
When all those people died,

My Mom was one among 'em.
For years I cried and cried.

A little red Volkswagen
Seems a smaller price

Than thousands of our people
We had to sacrifice...

Yet, giving up my beetle,
And all that it derives,

Is just a little bit of proof
That fear touches our lives.

My little red
Volkswagen

Is being sold
Today.

Our stocks and bonds
Are plummeting,

And we must
Find a way,

To keep up our enjoyment
Of travel 'cross the land.

Why our money's dwindling,
I do not understand.

Our finance girl advised us,
"Lower all you spend.

One thousand less each payday
Will make your problem end."

So I gave up
My little car,

And I'm
A little sad.

It made me smile,
When I was blue.

I guess it's
Not that bad...

Thousands
Of our people

Died upon
That day.

Their families
Really miss them.

We really
Had to pay!

Because of all
That happened,

We spend less
And we pray.

Most of us
Lost money

That we had
Put away.

So we will have
Less money,

As hard as
It may seem.

We'll hold our heads
Up high,

And enjoy
The American Dream...

When
We aren’t
Sharing our love
With each other,

We
Are wasting
Our time.

Hello Mom,

Do you want to go to Glenwood with us?

No. I feel bad.

Well, would you rather feel bad at home, or in Glenwood?

(She smiled) I guess I'd rather feel bad in Glenwood...

(Dennis' invitation)

A Little Slice of Heaven

(What Greg and Kathy might say)

A little slice of Heaven
(We've worked so very hard)
All around is peacefulness –
With God our only guard.

Nineteen acres
Full of bliss,
We earned
The right to say,

"Thank you God
For this, our home,
Where we can
Laugh and play."

We hear a frog,
Or maybe three.
It's fun
For us to know,

That they are still
A treasure.
Our hearts are
All aglow.

A little slice
Where God lives –
He had a
Humorous mind.

To make a frog
That sounds that way,
He must be
Oh so kind!

We find few words
When up the hill,
We see
Our humble abode.

Our home is just
So beautiful –
Complete
With frog and toad.

Sitting here
Down by the pond
We hear
A big fish swim.

Our fam' is
All excited,
And happy
To the brim!

Along comes
Cousin Dennis,
With twinkles
In his eye.

He wants to eat
Some fish tonight,
But just can't
Watch them die...

Catch and release
Little ones –
(Not because
He's nice).

He lets them go
So they can grow.
This is his
Advice.

Then you'll have
A mighty feast
From just one
Lovely fish.

Because it will
Be big enough
For you to
Fill your dish.

So God please
Bless our cousin,
And his woman
Pat.

Let them not
Eat all our fish!
For they will gain
More fat!

So, here we are
Dear Lord –
The fam'
Who lives with you.

We are forever
Thankful
For miracles
That you do.

This place
That we call home
Is just
A slice of heaven.

It's candy
To our eyes,
As if we all
Were seven...

'My' Dennis

'My' Dennis has been the wind beneath my wings for many years. He lifts me way up high with his love, and I never knew that I, in turn, lifted *him*.

Here he is,
Flying right by my side!
Here he is,
With a wink in his eye!

Letting me know,
As he flies by,
My love 'neath *his* wings
Is lifting *him* high!

I smile to myself,
And whisper a sigh,
"I didn't know
Turkeys could fly..."

(Smile...)

People are not to be

The 'whom' you think
they should be.

It isn't up to you.
It isn't up to me.

By
'My' Dennis

Just One of Those Days

I sit here very lonely! Though I have friends out there, I have been alone all day. Yet, I have been busy with this and that.

My illness is a lonely one. Today I stayed inside, while Dennis took care of some business.

Writing how I feel is difficult today. I'm afraid it won't be accurate, and I don't want to share secrets right now.

I want to bask in all I have learned, and feel good about where I am. I want to feel smart, and know there a lot of people who love me.

I want to pick up the telephone, call a friend, and talk two hours at a time.

When my Mom was alive, we would talk about anything and everything. We would have the 2-hour talks I'm missing now...

Maybe I'm alone and not lonely. There is a difference. I did give myself a pedicure, and I put my feet up for 20 minutes. I made some soup and cornbread, and I exercised a bit.

I must go outside and walk – whether I am afraid or not... I don't know what there is to fear.

I guess I fear the people out there.

I fear my symptoms, like when I know something happens, and others say it isn't happening at all.

How would you like to be in a red room and everyone says the room is blue?

How would you like to crash emotionally, when a certain kind of music plays?

How would you feel, if you wanted to help the world, and some days you can't, because of confusion in your thoughts?

While grasping for an idea that will make me feel better, I think of an idea by Ron Markovich. He said, "Recovery is a person living a life bigger than their illness."

Looking at my life, from this perspective, has often made me feel better. For I know that I live a life bigger than my fears, bigger than my rage, and bigger than my so-called, unreal thinking.

In short, I live a life bigger than my illness.

Thank you, Ron... This is a good thing you've shared with us.

People Who Have Died

I'm in my other way of thinking. Today, I am aware of people who have supposedly died.

I've been seeing my Mom around the metro area. She died 3½ years ago, and seeing her was very scary!

A friend committed suicide last April. In my mind, he is not really dead. He just made arrangements, to exit his old life, and live a better life elsewhere.

I had a wonderful therapist since 1981. When she died, I had similar thoughts about her. I just can't seem to let people go. I can't seem to let them die...

I never really experienced very many deaths in my life. After age 10, when Mom & we kids left Daddy, I experienced very few deaths. When aunts and uncles or cousins died, we never knew it, and we had access to only Mom's parents – no cousins on Mom's side were available.

All this may be why, in later life, I can't accept that people really truly die. Another therapist told me that mentally keeping people alive, when they have really died, is a form of grieving.

It's a way of getting through something very scary, and some say, very final.

I thought my behavior, in this matter, was from my illness. Yet, a person I trust told me that my thinking in this way comes only from sorrow and grief.

I thought my symptoms were flooding in, and that I was going out of reality.

Yet, it seems that reality is stranger than anything my 'other' brain can create, and, for me, the one good thing about death is that it is real...

Like A Butterfly

The echoing of memories
Going through my brain –

It causes such anxiety,
And causes mortal pain.

When I woke up this morning,
I stumbled 'gainst the wall.

With memories of yesterday,
That almost made me fall.

I fear I have no words to tell.
'Bout how it really was,

To tell you about yesterday,
And share with you the cause.

Some form of a dispiriting
Made me hurt real bad,

Made me feel so very scared,
And oh so very sad…

Dealing with what happens
Inside this brain of mine,

Whether it is real or not
I'd really like to find,

A way to stop the hurting
Way down deep in me,

A way to rid myself of rage,
How peaceful it would be…

If I should find the answer,
Of war that's in my brain,

If I could just describe it,
The awful mental pain,

Then I could help another,
Before my time is gone.

If I could find the root of this,
Then life could be a song.

I'd be just like a butterfly
Going here and there,

Doing things important,
And having strength to share.

If my difficulty
Could be all talked to death,

Then all my years of therapy
Were not a waste of breath.

Everything Will Be Alright

Dear Char,

I have had your question, on my mind, while out on the road.

I had you on my mind on the East Coast, and south of there.

You've been on my mind in the Ozarks and other places we've been this spring.

I guess the question of how the Super Humans came about is in a speech I've been giving. It might be written elsewhere...

It appears that the origin of the Super Humans cannot be told, because I don't know what it is...

I can only say that, at infancy, there were scary people standing much taller than me. They had my life and death in their hands, but they fought real hard and were very insecure and unstable at the same time.

By providing food, shelter, and clothes, they kept me cooing, and thinking everything would be alright.

They kept me from the boogieman, but at times, they *were* the boogieman...

Many times they would start to divorce and Daddy would break in the door at any moment.

There would be loud screaming, and scuffling noises. This has made me believe in the boogieman even now.

You now know that these very big and tall, insecure people were my parents...

During my growing years, the Super Humans stayed down in the caverns of my ridged mind.

Then there was New York...

After living there one or two years, I sought help, and was hospitalized for the first time. Here is where the Super Humans came back on a conscious level.

A girl at the hospital taught me how to get secret messages from the staff. She would show me scraps of paper, and find meaning from them.

At this hospital, during the three months I stayed there, I learned many ways of communicating without speaking.

I found messages in colors, others talking and noises in building walls. I thought people were trying to change me for the better. Now it feels like persecution...

I now have forgiven Mom and Dad for anything they may have done to hurt me.

I realized that I forgave them for being 'only human'. Then I realized, I was only human too. Then everyone on the planet was forgiven for the same reason.

Equality became even more clear in my heart and mind.

I only feel less smart, and less strong, when Super Humans appear...

My parents were the beginning of the Super Humans. I know that now. My mind registered them as the strongest most powerful humans in the world. They scared me, but they gave me what I needed to survive.

So, when I was nineteen years of age, this responsibility was somehow passed to other people in the world. I still feel very scared sometimes, when the Super Humans come around. Yet, I also know, for good or for bad, that when they are near, 'Everything will be alright'...

Love, your friend,

Pat

Dear Pat,

Now I think I understand a little better. Thank you for taking the time to write to me about the Super Humans and their origin. As I was reading what you wrote, I was sort of reminded of Stockholm Syndrome, the thing that happens to hostages when they are mistreated, but they bond to their captors, because these people are all they have to depend upon for food, water and the other needs of life.

That you are able to forgive and see that we are all just human, is part of being set free to go on with your work of reaching out to others with mental illness and the issues

that played a part in their origin...and to their friends and families. As Louise Hay puts it, "We are all victims of victims, and we can't teach what we haven't been taught." You were taught in a very hurtful and harsh way sometimes, seeing and experiencing things no child should have to be subjected to, but because of your frame of reference, you are able to help other people with mental illness, and the world will be a better place for your having been a part of it.

I am proud to have you as my friend.

Love, char

WELCOME
LOVE
TRUTH
RESPECT

Speech for A.M.H.C. Board Members

Dear Reader Most Kind,

I have a speech coming up.

I will be speaking to 32 Aurora

Mental Health board members,

about my life with mental illness.

In the next few pages, you will

be reading that speech.

SHARING AND CARING

To Whom It May Concern:

It was a bit of a challenge, thinking about speaking to all of you tonight. Yet, I said yes... It appears that, when I am just sharing and caring, I have fewer butterflies in my stomach.

With 37 years of therapy, I have learned many things. One is that I can go back into my past, and revisit anything and everything, without pain. There was a lot of pain back then...

I was born in Denver in 1948. I have two memories at 2 years of age.

One was a train ride to California during one of my parent's divorce attempts. The other was my need to take care of my Mom, starting with my covering her with a blanket.

I always thought my Mom was going to die, because my parents would have outrageous battles! They would separate, and Daddy would break open the door in the middle of the night. There would be screaming and scuffling noises.

Many, many times we would run out into the night in our pajamas. Dad would be taken away by police, but the next morning Mom and Dad would be in bed together...

I remember a time when I was ill. I was sleeping on the couch in the living room, and heard screaming. I opened my eyes to find my Dad on top of my Mom. He was hurting her by pulling at each side of her mouth with his thumbs!

I also started to scream. This was when he came after me.
Mom yelled at him, and he went back to her... That was the night he whipped my little sister with a half-inch wide stick. She wasn't even 5 years old! He usually didn't hit his kids – just our Mom.

On my Dad's side of the family was my Grandma and Grandpa Holley.

They always had that Black Jack Gum, licorice, or ice cream with jelly on it. We loved to go there, and my Grandma was very special to me.

Grandma Holley also had a tremor, but she would never spill a drop of anything she served us. I got my tremor from her through Daddy.

Grandma and Grandpa had a huge tree with a big swing hanging from it. We kids spent eternities swinging and playing in that back yard.

We spent time with my cousins, and aunts and uncles on Dad's side.

At Mom and Dad's final divorce, I was 10 years old. Mom called her parents to come get us. We snuck away, in the middle of the night, while Daddy was still at work. We took only a trunk of pictures and little else. There were 3 adults, and 4 children, in that old jalopy. So we could not take much. My Mom also bought a gun. She was so afraid of my Dad...

Meanwhile, most of the people I knew just fell away! If I have abandonment issues, it is partially due to this. None of Dad's side of the family came to see us.

Mom got a night job as a waitress. There was more abandonment, and little guidance. I felt extremely alone.
There was no one to watch us, so we watched each other. My older sister tried to discipline us with a belt, but it didn't take. We grew up wild. We ate as much sugared foods as we wanted, and there was always soda pop. We could have as much as we wanted, because Mom was not there to teach us portion control. I think Mom also wanted to justify her wine purchases, so she bought us pop and ice cream.

Jan, my closest sister, and I were inseparable. We fought and got into mischief.

At times, we pulled each other's hair out. My new, little, tom-boy girlfriend would protect me from Jan. She turned out to be a bit tougher than Jan, but Jan and I still loved each other. We also needed each other...

Janice wore this white skirt to school almost every day. It was just about all the clothes she had. One day someone poured black ink on it! Janice was devastated!

She and I stole candy, cigarettes, fabric and dresses. I also would make 'instant' dresses the night before school! They were just sack dresses but they worked out alright. Yet my conscience really hurt about the stealing.

Even these days I am very conscientious about my purchases...

I didn't know it then but I was popular in school. I was head cheerleader. My teacher said she never counted so many votes!

I still had no guidance, and I became conceited. The kids stopped liking me, until I changed back to my old self. As a sophomore, I became class representative. I was popular again. We moved out of town three months later...

I never felt really safe or nurtured, and guidance was still not to be found. Dad tried to take us a summer or two, but that effort fizzled out as well...

I met this young man when I was 14 years of age. People told me he was a heart breaker, but I didn't listen. We started a strange kind of interest in each other, and I would sneak out to see him.

By this time, I had a step Dad. He was great at first, but then we found out he was a liar. It appears that he had a family elsewhere.

He and I had a bad fight. I walked, in the dark, to the sister of this young man I spoke of.

You can probably guess what happened next. We ended up alone in his car. I became the victim of a hideous rape!

I told no one 'till years later, and I was never the same...

Shortly after the rape, I traveled a bit. I ended up in New York, where I danced in a chorus line at the famous Copa Cabana. I met many famous people, and actually accused Frankie Valli of being from the Rolling Stones. I smile at this.

He called me at the Rehearsal Club, where I was living. He said I had all I needed to make it big in showbiz. I agreed with him, and added, "Everything but talent"! We both laughed.

They tell me I have a mental illness.

It appears to me, that the lack of safety and guidance caused me to manifest the concept of Super Humans. When they are around, I feel horrible emotional pain, but I feel as if everything will be ok at the same time (much like my childhood)... It's like being in a room, getting scared and slipping into another room for protection.

About a year after the Copa, I was hospitalized for the first time. This was also the first appearance of Super Humans...
I was there 3 months. They put wires on my head as I slept.
They gave me tranquilizers, and made me stay awake.

A fellow patient taught me how to find hints left by the staff.

Once she showed me a torn piece of paper, and proceeded to tell me that particular message. It was a gum wrapper... I was now on my way. I started making meanings out of various things. I once heard a nurse counting patients. When she got to the number 10, I thought I was suppose to get my phone dime from that patient! He just said that he wasn't a bank... So much for that...

In 1971, I came home to Colorado, and lived with my Mom in a two room apartment. She was suffering from a mental illness like I was. Yet she gave me the only bed in that little apartment. It was all made up with clean white sheets, and it was heaven!

I was so sick, and this was a grand gift I will never forget!

Then, I moved into this house, where I had to be doing something positive – like going to school. I went to college and received a degree in Recreational Leadership.

I met 'my' Dennis, who lived in the high rise next door. We've been warriors together through a lot of bad times, but it is the good times that balanced the bad.

From the day we met, I just talked and talked. Dennis just listened and listened.

He seemed to like hearing whatever I had to say, and never seemed to judge me. We were like two peas in a pod…

Then, one day, his boss sent him to Utah to another branch of the company. I was devastated and ended up in the hospital for a third time.

I didn't detect Dennis' depression until we were married. He was working 72 hours per week, and he didn't even want to take a walk with me. I just figured he was tired.

About 5 years passed, with my therapists asking what we were doing for fun. We weren't doing very much…

Dennis finally told me he wanted to die. This big strong man wanted to die... I immediately reached for the phone. I called Kaiser's Psychiatric Offices, and Dennis began eight very thorough years of therapy.

The first thing he was asked was if he wanted to end his marriage to me! He said, "No, she's good for me when she's well." I love Dennis, and still cringe when I think that maybe he could have said, "Yes, I want to end it."

Without our therapists, we would never have made it – even with both of us trying very hard. They helped us learn communication skills.

Without good communication, we would not have known how to recover from our disagreements. Our mental health professionals deserve a lot of credit for the longevity of our marriage.

We learned to have fun together. We did some camping. We took walks. We went out to dinner and had friends over to our house. In between there were my hospitalizations...

Our sense of humor, our mutual support, and our love for each other, has brought us through hard times.

Often, I went through hell alone, and 'my' Dennis did not know what he would find when he came home from work.

A lot of credit goes to him and his belief in God. Credit goes to me, because I fight like a warrior.

I don't miss any meetings with my mental health professionals, I take my medicine, and I manage my illness from day to day.

I have been in the pits of hell! I have spent many 'alone' hours being suicidal. I get messages in my body, and at times I have wanted to take a knife and cut away the part of me that was getting these messages.

I have mistaken hot coffee for
blood, bacon for tarantula meat,
and canned peaches for testicles.
I have watched the carpet turn
colors right before my eyes.

I have had the belief that my
vagina and anus were sewn shut,
and that the building I was in was
alive. This building was also a
spaceship, because the sun had
gone out, and we were going to
another galaxy for another sun...

Temporary sunshine was given to
me in the form of a yellow liquid.
It was really Thorazine – a
popular medicine used a long
time ago to treat mental illness.

When I have to go to the hospital, or half-way house, it feels like I am in a pressure cooker! No word can describe it except the word, "hell"... I always feel that I am the only patient, and everyone else there is working on me.

Sometimes, I don't know what city or state I am in! I don't trust newspapers or magazines – not even television or radio! For instance, I didn't believe the report, when we landed on the moon...

Yes, the cure is as painful as the symptoms. Yet, when it is over, I can face the world again.

It takes me months to recover from one of these 'crashes'. I have fought my way back so many times they can't be counted...

I have two brains that switch back and forth without warning. Sometimes, when this happens, I just act as if everything is ok, or I talk with Dennis, or I call my therapist.

There are times when my body loses strength and I must lie down under the covers. I lie there until I can connect with my therapist who has taken me to a place of possibility countless times.

My parents are dead now, and I will always love them. I was very fortunate to be close with my Mom for 30 years after New York. Yet, they did not raise and nurture me. Mental health professionals have been my source of caring, respect, and truth. I consider them to be somewhat like parents.

When I get suicidal, sometimes I get mad at 'my' Dennis, because he won't let me go... I see his pain, and I don't want to hurt him like that again...

I did attempt suicide once. This was about 20 years ago. I sat there with milk and pills. It was very frightening – taking pill after pill...

I spent that night unconscious in the emergency room. Later, 'my' Dennis walked in and I started crying. I told him I was sorry. He looked so very sad.

Later, my physician told me that I almost died – even with that stomach pump...

As for family, mine has been wounded! We have stayed away from each other a lot. My heart was so broken it was not healed until I was age 48. So, I've decided that fighting with my family is no longer how I want to spend my life.

'My' Dennis has been with me through about 20 hospitalizations. He says we would never have made it if it wasn't for my trying so hard. I say to him, "Ditto", because he worked very hard, also.

Dennis went through eight years of therapy for major depression, and also more therapy, to separate me from my illness. He finally realized that I was not my illness, and saw me as just a person who loved him very much. I just had some problems that didn't make sense... Not only this, but they were problems he learned he couldn't fix...

It helped our marriage, when I would do the bills and the checkbook. No matter if I was in the hospital or not, the bills would get done. While I was in the hospital, I was still able to support him. Sometimes I would encourage him to stay home and watch TV, because he would get very tired juggling work and visiting with me.

It still frustrates 'my' Dennis, when he cannot fix my pain, and my illness. Yet all I need from him is that wonderful trio, of Love, Respect and Truth. This is enough to last us an eternity...

I have found a better relationship with my higher power.

I have been cared about by literally thousands of mental health professionals.

My husband is a good human being, and I cherish our marriage.

I have written 10 books, and most of them are offered over the Barnes and Noble web site, bn.com.

They were all published by my company, "ITSMEEE" Industries.

"ITSMEEE" Industries is in the process of becoming a non-profit organization. We have a board of directors and 'My' Dennis is Chairman of the Board. I was elected Executive Director of the company.

My 9th book, "Walk a Mile in Our Shoes", displays 8 interviews of fellow mental health consumers.

This book will help erase stigma, by showing ways we are all equal. It also tells of how we are all unique. The importance of mental health services is also portrayed.

We do not claim to suffer any more than any other group of individuals. How can you measure? We just want things like stigma to go away, as with any illness.

The people interviewed are survivors and warriors. They are amazing people and they can laugh at the very thing that puts them at hell's door.

I really enjoyed their stories! I thought the interviews would be of my giving, but I received so much throughout the whole process...

"Walk a Mile in Our Shoes" was published in February of this year, and will be available for a suggested, tax deductible, contribution of 20 dollars. If any of you would like a copy, please stay after the meeting.

My story has been in the Rocky Mountain News, and recently, my biography has been entered into Who's Who in America of 2005. It appears, after all, that I will be able to give back the favor that I owe the world...

Helping one person is wonderful, but I want to reach millions!

I still find myself tortured by what happens to me. I still waste some time in pain. I still fight like that warrior I spoke of earlier, but now I also feel connected with other humans. I know that most are swimming just as hard as I am.

I have never hurt anyone in my 56 years on this planet, yet there is stigma directed toward me.

These days Dennis and I are sort of retired. With help from Aurora Mental Health and my meds, we are able to travel in our RV. We are together more, and we live a lot of life in abundance!

We see beauty everywhere in this country, and we can distribute "Walk a Mile in Our Shoes" by way of our RV.

My fifth book, "I Want to Live", has a section about many places in the country we have traveled. We've been to a lot of beaches, and they are mesmerizing! There are the Mammoth Caves, and Death Valley (where altitude is 225 feet *below* sea level)! The Grand Canyon is so mind boggling that we just can't take
it all in! It is so beautiful!

We enjoy talking to each other as we go down the road. We share our thoughts about the country side, memories we have, and anything we can think of.
This is such a joy to us both...

These days, we spend more time with Dennis' side of the family, and I seem to just fit right in. We had another dinner last time we were there. There were 24 of us, and I wasn't even nervous.
I caught myself feeling like just another member of the family!

These things are huge to me, because I was never able to blend in with people as well as now.

Something else amazing is that my sisters and I are gravitating toward each other after all these years! The three of us are having lunch soon, and there will be no one else there. I feel that my books have something to do with our healing, as I gave them a copy every time one came out.

I am seeing a world filled with miracles, and I have begun to feel safe. The fear I use to have is being reduced by meds and coping skills. I get so proud when I can control my symptoms with skills I have learned.

My mission in life is to cut through the 'stuff' to what really matters. I have dedicated the rest of my life to Caring, Respect, and Truth. These are my most valuable possessions, and I want to share them with you...

I now live a life bigger than my rage and bigger than my fear. In short, I live a life bigger than my illness.

I've been asked what took so
long for me to find my way.
I guess lots of things get better
with age – maybe even people…

Sincerely and With Love,
Patricia A. Fisher (Pat)